Looking after
Guinea Pigs

Laura Howell

Designed by Joanne Kirkby
Edited by Sarah Khan
Illustrations by Christyan Fox

Consultant: Karen Le Cras

Usborne Quicklinks

For links to carefully chosen websites where
you can find out more about guinea pigs, go to the
Usborne Quicklinks Website at www.usborne.com/quicklinks
and enter the keywords **"pet guides guinea pigs"**

There you'll find links to websites where you can:

- Discover the right pet for you
- Watch video clips on how to care for guinea pigs
- Solve quizzes and find fun things to make and do
- Find fascinating facts about guinea pigs

Contents

About guinea pigs

Guinea pigs, also known as cavies, are small, hairy animals which originally came from South America. They make gentle and friendly pets, as long as you look after them.

This book will help you choose a guinea pig, and tell you how to take care of it.

A guinea pig's tail is too short to see.

The ears are small, and fold over a little.

The back paws have three toes, but the front ones have four.

This guinea pig has short hair, but there are long-haired varieties, too.

In the family

Guinea pigs aren't related to pigs, but belong to a family of animals called rodents that have long teeth for gnawing. Mice and rats are rodents.

A guinea pig uses its strong teeth to gnaw food and chew on hay.

What's in a name?

No one knows for sure how guinea pigs got their odd name. Some people think it's because they were brought to Europe via Guinea, in Africa.

How big?

Guinea pigs don't grow very large. An average adult guinea pig is around 25cm (10in) long, and weighs about 1.25kg (2$\frac{1}{2}$lb). They live for up to seven years.

Seeing

Guinea pigs are good at spotting movement, but can't see details well. Their eyes are high on their heads, so they see things above them best.

Don't make sudden noises near your guinea pig, as they might cause it to panic.

Hearing

A guinea pig's sensitive ears can hear many sounds that yours can't.

Smelling

A guinea pig's keen sense of smell helps it to identify friends and enemies, or to tell if it's in an area that belongs to another animal.

A guinea pig will sniff you to learn your scent and to recognize you.

SNIFF...

Eating machines

In the wild, guinea pigs spend up to 20 hours every day munching grass.

This guinea pig is enjoying some cabbage.

Your guinea pig will want to spend a lot of time eating and chewing hay.

Living together

Wild guinea pigs live in groups called herds. Each herd has one male guinea pig, called a boar, and many females, called sows.

Guinea pigs feel safer in a group than on their own.

7

Choosing a guinea pig

Guinea pig babies are ready to leave their mother when they are about five or six weeks old. Here are some things to look for when choosing your new pet.

There should be a bald patch behind each ear.

The eyes should be bright, not sticky or cloudy.

Check that its teeth are clean and straight-edged.

The nose should be dry.

Make sure the hair is glossy.

Its body should feel plump, not bony.

Where to buy

You can buy guinea pigs from pet stores, but it's better to buy from breeders. Guinea pig shelters also have pets that need new homes.

Choose the most friendly and inquisitive guinea pigs, especially if you are getting them from a shelter.

How many?

Guinea pigs get lonely very easily, so you should buy a pair. If you buy two that don't already know each other, they may fight, so it's best to get two that are already friends.

If you buy a male and a female, they should have had an operation that stops them from having babies.

What breed?

Long-haired guinea pigs have flowing, silky hair that grows down to the floor.

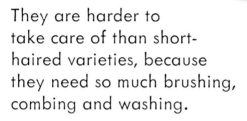

They are harder to take care of than short-haired varieties, because they need so much brushing, combing and washing.

Long-haired guinea pigs need grooming at least once a day.

Short-haired guinea pigs are most commonly kept as pets, because they are easy to keep clean. They can have many different markings.

Adult Abyssinian guinea pigs have "rosettes" — short, flower-shaped tufts of hair.

How to choose

Watch all the guinea pigs
from a little way away.
Don't try to touch them yet.

*Try to stay
quiet while you
watch the guinea pigs.*

*All guinea
pigs have
different
personalities.*

Look for the most lively
guinea pig. Ask if you
can be shown how to
pick it up.

zzz

Hold it and gently stroke
it for a while. Decide if
you think it's friendly.

*It's a good idea to sit down
while you hold the guinea pig,
in case it struggles and falls.*

What will I need?

Before you bring your guinea pigs home, have the things they'll need ready for them. You can buy all of these things from a pet store.

Carrying box

You'll need a box big enough for two guinea pigs to carry your new pets home. This can be made of cardboard or plastic, but make sure it's sturdy and has air holes so the animals can breathe.

This pet-carrying box has its lid partly open, so you can see inside.

Put a sheet of paper and some hay in the bottom of the box.

Which home?

The type of home you buy will depend on where you're going to keep it. You'll need a cage for indoors, or a hutch for outside. Find out more on pages 16–19 and 32–35.

Bedding

Guinea pigs need something to burrow in, such as clean, shredded paper or bedding from a pet store. Avoid wood shavings or sawdust, as these can cause health problems.

Pet stores sell bags of shredded paper, or you can shred some yourself.

Use newspaper or large sheets of plain paper to line the floor of your pet's hutch or cage.

If you buy bedding from a store, make sure the label says it's safe for guinea pigs.

Water

If you put water in a bowl, it will quickly become dirty. Instead, use a drip-feed bottle that attaches to the side of the cage.

Don't let the spout's end touch the hay and bedding, or it will leak.

Hang the water bottle at a comfortable height for your guinea pig, as shown here.

Hay

Guinea pigs need to chew on hay to stay healthy and keep their teeth worn down. Scatter some over the bedding. You can also put a little in a hayrack attached to the hutch's door.

Reaching up and having a tug of war with a strand of hay is good exercise.

There are many varieties of hay but meadow hay is best to scatter over the bedding. Guinea pigs will love burrowing in, playing in, and then eating soft, fresh meadow hay. You can buy this type of hay from pet stores.

Feeding dish

Buy a small, ceramic bowl for your guinea pig's food. Don't use plastic ones, as they are easy to knock over and are likely to get chewed.

This kind of heavy ceramic food bowl is suitable for guinea pigs to use.

Hutches and arks

Although they are small animals, guinea pigs need lots of space in which to sleep, run and play. The best home for a pet guinea pig is a hutch or a large cage.

These two pages tell you about keeping guinea pigs outside in a hutch.

The roof should be covered in felt, and sloping at an angle to keep moisture from gathering on top.

A wire mesh door lets in light and fresh air.

The hutch needs a separate area where your guinea pig can sleep and hide away in peace.

If your hutch has short legs, stand it on bricks to raise it higher.

Size and position

Two guinea pigs need a hutch at least 120cm (4ft) wide and 60cm (2ft) tall. For every additional guinea pig you have, add another 30cm (1ft) in length.

Put the hutch in a shed that's not too damp, hot or cold, and is protected from the wind. It must be raised off the ground so that cats, foxes and other animals can't open the door.

Preparing the hutch

Line the floor of the hutch with large sheets of paper, then spread bedding around 5cm (2in) deep on top. Finally, add a large clump of hay.

You must change your guinea pigs' bedding at least twice a week, and their hay every day, or they will become smelly.

A grazing ark

You should let your pets out to run around and nibble grass in a wooden grazing ark whenever the weather is dry and warm. The ark should be at least 180cm (6ft) long by 120cm (4ft) wide.

Never leave your guinea pigs alone for a long time in an ark, as dangerous animals might try to get in while you're not looking.

Put a little food and a full water bottle in the ark.

Wire mesh sides let in air and stop your pets from escaping.

Grazing arks have a covered area away from the sun and rain. Add a little hay so your guinea pigs can sleep there if they want.

Setting up

Place the ark in an area that is sheltered from the wind and sun, and where there is healthy grass to eat.

Avoid putting the ark over any flowers, such as buttercups or poppies. Most flowers are poisonous to guinea pigs.

If you think your pet has eaten something poisonous, take it to the vet straight away.

Return your guinea pigs to the hutch at the end of the day. Move the ark to a fresh patch of grass, ready for tomorrow.

Settling in

Your guinea pigs might be scared if they're leaving their mothers for the first time. They will need help to settle into their new home.

Getting ready

Before you bring your pets home, have fresh bedding, hay, food and water ready in their cage.

Leave your guinea pigs alone for the first day so they can get used to the unfamiliar sights and smells.

Arranging their bedding makes the guinea pigs feel more at home.

Taming

Guinea pigs that are never handled become nervous around people. After your pets have settled in, you should try to get them used to your scent, voice and touch.

Help your guinea pigs get used to you by offering them a snack in your hand.

The more time you spend together, the friendlier they will become.

Picking up

When a guinea pig is used to you, try picking it up. Gently place one hand underneath its body, supporting its bottom with your other hand. Lift it up and hold it close to you.

Happy, contented guinea pigs usually make gurgling noises as you pet them.

GURGLE...
GURGLE...

Feeling safe

A relaxed guinea pig will sit in your lap or cuddle up to your chest. If it starts to struggle or squeal, carefully put it back in its cage.

If your guinea pig is happy to be picked up, stroke it gently as you hold it.

Meeting friends

When your guinea pig has become used to you and your home, try introducing it to your family and friends. Show them the right way to pick up and hold a guinea pig first.

Young children should hold a guinea pig near floor level, for safety.

Other pets

Keep your guinea pigs away from other kinds of pets. Even if the other pets are friendly, they might hurt your guinea pigs accidentally.

Dogs and cats frighten guinea pigs, so keep them apart.

If you already have a guinea pig and want to buy another, take yours to help choose the new one, so you know that your two pets will get along.

Two guinea pigs will say hello by nudging and sniffing each other.

Feeding

Guinea pigs need to eat a variety of dried and fresh food. Start off giving your pet the same kind of food it had before you bought it, then try introducing it to new kinds.

Dried food

Pet stores sell dry pellets for guinea pigs that are full of things they need, such as vitamins and minerals.

Keep dried food fresh by storing it in a container with a lid.

Make sure the food doesn't contain any artificial ingredients.

Don't buy any other kinds of rodent foods, as they're too large and firm for guinea pigs to digest.

COUGH
COUGH

How much?

Feed your guinea pigs dried food once a day, and fresh food twice a day.

Guinea pigs don't hoard food, so they need a fresh supply every day.

Whenever you feed your guinea pig, fill the food bowl to the top. It will only eat as much food as it needs. As long as it gets lots of exercise, it won't become too fat.

A guinea pig will eat until it's full. If it leaves lots of food, give it less the next day.

25

Grazing

Guinea pigs love to graze on fresh grass.
To make sure they get what they need,
feed them grass picked by hand or let
them out in a grazing ark (see page 18).

In spring, only let your guinea pigs out to
graze for a short amount of time. Spring
grass is very rich and can easily lead to
upset tummies.

Guinea pigs can safely eat a few
daisies as well as fresh grass.

Make sure the
grass is dry. Guinea
pigs can get poorly
if they get wet.

Hay

Hay is dried grass. A guinea pig needs to munch on it all day, so always provide plenty. It should be soft hay, with no sharp ends.

Don't worry if you see your guinea pig eating its droppings.

Droppings

Guinea pigs can't take all the goodness from food the first time they eat. They make soft droppings that they can eat and digest again.

Types of teeth

A guinea pig needs to thoroughly chew its food. Its front teeth are designed for biting food into pieces, and the strong back teeth mash it up.

There's a gap behind a guinea pig's front teeth, where food is held before it's chewed up.

Fresh foods

Wild guinea pigs are herbivores, which means they eat plants, but not meat. You must feed your pet vegetables, grass, and a little fruit along with dried food.

Eat your greens

Your guinea pigs need leafy green vegetables, such as broccoli and kale, every day. Iceberg lettuce and any type of spinach apart from baby spinach can cause upset tummies.

A pair of guinea pigs need around 50g (2oz) of vegetables every morning and evening.

Vitamin C

Guinea pigs need to eat foods that are rich in vitamin C. Without it, they develop a skin disease called scurvy. Dried guinea pig food usually has added vitamin C, but the best source is leafy green vegetables.

Many fruits also contain vitamin C. You can give a little fruit as a treat from time to time.

Here are some fruits and vegetables that your guinea pigs might enjoy.

Banana

Watermelon

Brussels sprouts

Grapes

Broccoli

Pear

Make sure all the fresh foods you give are clean. Never give sweet things such as chocolate, as this will make a guinea pig sick.

Preparing fresh food

Wash the fruit
and vegetables
to get rid of
any chemicals.
Carefully cut it into
slices or chunks.

If you feed your pets at
the same times every day,
they will learn when to
expect a meal.

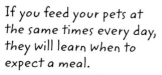

Every morning
and evening,
give your guinea
pigs fresh food
in a clean
feeding bowl.

Before bedtime,
throw away any
uneaten food.
If it starts to rot,
it could make
your guinea
pigs sick.

New food

Some guinea pigs are fussy eaters. Don't make any sudden changes to a guinea pig's diet. When you give it a type of food it hasn't tried before, only offer a small amount. It will sniff it to find out if it is good to eat.

This guinea pig is deciding if it likes carrots.

If your guinea pig ignores the new food or doesn't eat much of it, it probably doesn't like it.

An indoor guinea pig

A guinea pig that lives indoors is more likely
to stay healthy than one that is kept outside.
Indoor guinea pigs still need exercise and
regular grazing time in an ark, though.

A guinea pig cage

A pair of guinea pigs needs a cage at least 60
x 120cm (2 x 4ft) in size. The cage should have
a plastic bottom, lined with paper and bedding
in the same way as a hutch (see page 16).

Change the water in the
water bottle every day.

You can keep some of your
pets' hay fresh for longer by
putting it in a hayrack.

Give your guinea pigs
a hiding place inside the cage ----→
or cover part of the cage with a towel.

Where to put the cage

Guinea pigs can make a lot of noise, so don't keep the cage in your bedroom, or your pets will wake you up in the night.

Put the cage in a place where the surrounding area is easy to clean, such as the corner of the room.

Guinea pigs like to kick their bedding through the bars.

Keep the cage away from:
- radiators and fires
- direct sunlight
- windows and doors
- damp places
- TVs, radios and stereos
- other pets

Loud noises frighten guinea pigs, so keep your pets' cage in a quiet spot.

Spotting dangers

When you let your guinea pigs out of their cage to exercise, check the room beforehand for possible dangers.

Don't let your guinea pigs near any objects that are hot or sharp.

Don't let your pets run loose on a high table, as they might fall over the side.

Guinea pigs will chew anything, so keep electric wires out of their reach.

Put houseplants where your guinea pigs can't nibble them. They could be poisonous.

Eating a houseplant could make your guinea pig sick, or even kill it.

Toilet habits

Guinea pigs usually go to the toilet in one corner of their cage, but it's a good idea to put newspaper on the floor before letting them out.

If your guinea pig has an accident, wipe the spot clean with a warm, soapy cloth.

Watch out

Warn everyone in your family that your guinea pigs are loose, so no one accidentally steps on them. Keep the door of the room closed.

Your pets might run in different directions, so watch them closely.

Play and exercise

Guinea pigs are playful and curious animals with lots of energy, so they need plenty of exercise and playtime.

Pet stores sell toys for guinea pigs, although household objects, such as boxes with holes cut in them, also provide hours of fun.

You can make an obstacle course like this one to keep your guinea pigs amused.

Guinea pigs will crawl into and climb over tubes, boxes and cushions.

Guinea pig toys

Don't give your guinea pig toys designed for other animals, such as cats, as they might chew them up and choke on the small parts.

A toy as simple as a paper bag or cardboard tube stuffed with hay will be enjoyable for your guinea pigs.

Rubbing

A guinea pig sometimes rubs against things to mark them with a scent that other guinea pigs can smell, but you can't.

Any area with this scent is the guinea pig's territory, which means it's a place where it feels safe.

Guinea pigs rub their chins or bottoms against things to mark them as theirs.

Jumping for joy

Sometimes guinea pigs leap straight up, arching their back, or run across the floor and make a series of shorter jumps.

Wooo...

This is called popcorn jumping, and it's the sign of a healthy and happy guinea pig.

Running around

A guinea pig needs regular exercise to keep it healthy. Let your guinea pigs out of their hutch or cage at least three times a week.

Put your pets in a run, grazing ark or any enclosed place where they can't escape.

Catching your pet

When your guinea pig has finished playing or exercising, you'll need to return it to its home for a rest.

Leave the hutch door open with a ramp down to the ground.

Your guinea pig might come back in by itself.

Guinea pigs are easily tempted by fresh fruit.

If your pet doesn't want to return to its hutch, or you can't wait, try coaxing it in with a tasty snack.

Don't shout at your pet, or chase after it. A frightened guinea pig is less likely to come to you.

Housekeeping

To keep your guinea pigs healthy, you should clean out their cage or hutch two or three times a week, and keep their bedding fresh.

Dirty bedding

Most guinea pigs use a corner of their living area as a toilet. If the bedding becomes soggy or smelly in this area, remove it and replace it with a fresh handful each day.

Wrap smelly old bedding in newspaper before you throw it away.

This guinea pig is having fun tearing up its new bedding.

Cage cleaning

Empty the used bedding and any old food out of your guinea pigs' cage, then wash the food bowl, water bottle and parts of the cage.

Use disinfectant that's safe for guinea pigs. You can buy this in a pet store.

Rinse everything thoroughly, making sure there are no dirty bits left behind. Dry everything with an old towel.

Keep an old towel especially for drying your guinea pigs' things.

41

Hutch cleaning

Throw away the hay, old bedding and paper. Use a spatula or dustpan and brush to remove the dirt.

Dip a brush into some warm, soapy water. Scrub the inside of the hutch and rinse it with clean water.

Let the hutch dry. Spray it with disinfectant. Lay paper in the bottom, then cover it with fresh bedding and hay.

Make sure you use a guinea pig-friendly disinfectant from a pet store.

Scrub the water bottle with soapy water. Rinse it well. Wash your hands after you've finished.

Use a bottle brush to scrub the water bottle.

Out of the way

While you're cleaning your guinea pigs' home, put your pets in a run, grazing ark or any enclosed place where they can't escape.

It's a good idea to clean your guinea pigs' home while they're out grazing.

What does it mean?

Guinea pigs make a variety of sounds and use body language to let each other know how they feel.

If you watch your pets and listen carefully to them, you will soon be able to understand what they're trying to say.

Sniffing

A guinea pig learns a lot from its keen sense of smell.

This guinea pig is "nasal gazing" — sniffing the air to find out what's going on.

When guinea pigs meet for the first time, they sniff each other to decide if they are friends.

Making noises

Guinea pigs use a wide range of noises to express themselves.

A happy guinea pig purrs, or makes a soft chortling noise.

CHORTLE

SQUEEEAK

An unhappy guinea pig will make a loud, high-pitched squeak.

A rumbling sound means your guinea pig is annoyed. If you are handling it when it does this, put it down.

WHEEEK!

RUMBLE

When guinea pigs are excited, they give out a loud "wheeek!"

PURR PURR

Male guinea pigs "rumblestrut" when they want to show off. They sway their hips while making a low purr.

Fighting

Guinea pigs can get angry with each other. Before they fight, they will fluff out their hair and make an angry chattering sound. They then bare their teeth in a wide yawn.

You can stop guinea pigs from attacking each other by throwing a towel over them.

Under a towel, guinea pigs get confused and stop fighting.

If a pair of guinea pigs has had a fight, they must be kept in separate cages afterwards.

Once two guinea pigs have had a fight, they will not make friends again.

Mysterious chirps

A guinea pig might stand still and make a chirping noise for several minutes. No one but the guinea pig knows what this means.

All other guinea pigs nearby will stop and listen if a companion starts to chirp.

CHIRP CHIRP

Staying still

A scared guinea pig will stand still. If your guinea pig is frozen in fear, leave it until it starts to move again, or you might scare it more.

When a wild guinea pig sees a dangerous animal, it freezes like this. Standing still makes it harder to spot.

Baby guinea pigs

When they are a few months old, guinea pigs are ready to have babies. Never try to breed guinea pigs without expert advice.

Newborn babies

Baby guinea pigs are called pups. A mother can have up to five pups at a time.

Baby guinea pigs are born with hair and open eyes, and can walk within an hour or two. They are about as big as an adult mouse.

This mother guinea pig will lick her newborn babies clean.

Mealtime

At first, the pups drink milk from their mother. She only has two nipples, so they must take turns. After a few days, the pups start to eat dry foods.

The smallest pup might struggle to get enough milk from its mother.

BAAAA!

Helpful aunties

In the wild, a mother guinea pig is surrounded by her sisters and cousins, who will help to raise her young. These other females protect the pups.

Guinea pig pups are cared for by many members of their family.

Happy families

At two weeks old, the pups play together, and huddle up for warmth. If a young pup is separated from its family, it will become anxious and look for them.

The pups make a "hut hut hut" noise to let their sisters and brothers know where they are.

HUT...
HUT...

Mini adults

Guinea pigs are fully grown at one year old, but they look like adults much sooner than this.

This guinea pig is the mother, and all the others on these two pages are her month-old pups.

50

Leaving home

Male guinea pigs should be kept in separate cages from their mother and sisters when they reach three weeks old. If not, they will fight or try to make more babies.

Female pups can stay with their mother.

One male pup can go and live in a separate cage with its father when it's a few weeks old.

51

Grooming

Guinea pigs are clean animals, and groom themselves. You can help keep your pets in good condition by brushing and washing them.

Before you groom and wash your guinea pig, make sure you have all of these things:

- soft brush
- large plastic bowl
- jug of warm (NOT hot) water
- shampoo for guinea pigs (you can buy this from a pet store or vet)
- towel
- hair dryer

This guinea pig is grooming itself by licking its paws.

Brushing

Put down a towel for your guinea pig to sit on while it is being brushed.

Get your guinea pig in a comfortable position in your lap, or on a low surface.

Use one hand to keep your guinea pig still.

Brush the hair in the direction it grows.

Gently brush the hair on your guinea pig's back and bottom.

Longer-haired guinea pigs may have knots in their hair. Carefully untangle these.

Your guinea pig will enjoy being groomed, as long as you're gentle.

Bathing

Help keep your pet clean and healthy by giving it a bath every four to six weeks.

Hold your guinea pig firmly but gently.

Lower your guinea pig into a large, plastic bowl half-filled with warm (not hot) water.

Splash water on its coat. Pour a capful of shampoo onto its back, and gently rub it into the hair.

Don't get any shampoo in your guinea pig's eyes and nose.

Hold up your guinea pig's head as you pour the water.

Pour warm water over your guinea pig's neck, and rub it in. Keep pouring until all the shampoo has gone.

Drying off

After washing your guinea pig, lift it onto
a towel. Fold the towel over your pet and
rub its coat gently. Give it a thorough brush
afterwards. Make sure the room is warm.

*This guinea pig
is being towel
dried after
a bath.*

Dry your guinea pig's hair with a hair dryer,
making sure you use the lowest heat setting,
but not the cool air function. Hold the dryer a
little distance away from your pet – if it's too
close, your pet will become overheated.

Keeping healthy

Your guinea pig can't tell you when it's feeling unwell, so you must watch it carefully for signs that something is wrong. If you think your pet is ill, take it to the vet (see page 60).

Sore skin

Guinea pigs often suffer from skin infections. If bald, scaly or sore patches start to appear on your pet's body, take it to show the vet.

A guinea pig that bites or scratches itself like this might have a skin problem.

Mites and lice

A guinea pig that's scratching a lot could have mites or lice. These are little creatures that live in an animal's fur and make it itch. Mites are too tiny to see, but you might spot lice wriggling through your pet's hair.

Lice are very small. This drawing shows one bigger so you can see what its shape is like.

You can get rid of mites and lice using a medicated shampoo recommended by your vet.

Wear old gloves to put your guinea pig in its carrying box, and thoroughly clean its cage. Wash its hair with medicated shampoo. You'll need to wash all your other guinea pigs' hair too.

General health

Your guinea pig might be unwell if its breathing is wheezy, or if it doesn't want to eat or drink.

Take your pet to a vet if it doesn't get better by itself.

If a guinea pig is breathing heavily or has a runny nose and eyes, it might have a cold. It should be seen by a vet at once.

A guinea pig with a cold might develop a more serious illness, unless it receives treatment.

If your guinea pig is wounded, wash the wound with warm water and apply a little aloe vera gel.

Heatstroke

A guinea pig gets sick if it doesn't have shade in hot weather. If it is gasping and lying on its tummy, it might have heatstroke. Don't give it anything to drink while it's gasping, or it might choke.

Wrap your pet in a towel soaked with cold water then take it to the vet.

A guinea pig that is feeling unwell will need to rest.

Visiting the vet

If your guinea pig looks poorly, or needs its teeth or claws clipped, take it to a vet.

Contact a vet quickly if your pet's droppings are runny, or it can't breathe properly. These are both signs that it might be seriously sick.

Making the journey

Take your guinea pig to the vet in a carrying box with a little hay at the bottom.

To keep your ill guinea pig calm, take its friend to the vet too.

Keep the carrying box as still as you can while the car is moving.

In the car, put the box on an old blanket to avoid mess. At the vet, keep your guinea pigs in the box while you're waiting, so they won't be scared by the other animals at the clinic.

Here, a vet is using clippers to trim a guinea pig's claws. This doesn't hurt the guinea pig.

Claws and teeth

If your guinea pig is having difficulty running around, a vet may need to clip its claws.

Teeth can be clipped by a vet if they have become too long. Overgrown teeth make it hard for a guinea pig to eat.

Your guinea pig's teeth will probably not need clipping if you give it lots of good hay to eat.

Going away

If you are going away, ask a friend to look after your pets. Try to ask someone who already knows about guinea pigs.

Before you go

Tell your friend how much and how often to feed your guinea pigs, how to clean their cage, and how to recognize if they are unwell.

Give your friend the vet's number and a list of the things your pets need.

Getting to a friend

You will need to take your guinea pigs to your friend's house if he can't visit your home every day.

Give your friend everything that's needed to look after your pets.

Transport your guinea pigs in their carrying box.

Take food, bedding and cleaning equipment, along with the hutch or cage. Remember to wash them first.

This guinea pig is still getting the fresh foods it needs while its owner is away.

Other guinea pigs

If your friend has guinea pigs already, ask him not to mix them with yours. They might fight, or, if they are of opposite sexes, they might try to have babies.

Your guinea pigs will feel less nervous of their new surroundings if they have something with a familiar smell, such as a handful of old hay.

Index

Cover design by Kate Rimmer
Digital manipulation by Keith Furnival

Photo credits

(t-top, m-middle, b-bottom, l-left, r-right)
All photographs by Jane Burton, except
Front Cover b © Jane Burton/Warren Photographic Ltd; 23b © Jane Burton/Warren
Photographic Ltd; 32b © SAVIC; 38bl © Juniors Bildarchiv GmbH/Alamy;
43br © Juniors Bildarchiv GmbH/Alamy; 52b © Jane Burton/Warren Photographic Ltd